All Shards & Paste

Joey Poetry

Published by Scorched Feathers
Cleveland, Ohio, USA

Copyright © 2019 Joanna "Joey" Polisena

All rights reserved. No part of this publication may be reproduced, distributed, or transmitted in any form or by any means, including photocopying, recording, or other electronic or mechanical methods, without the prior written permission of the publisher, except in the case of brief quotations embodied in critical reviews and certain other noncommercial uses permitted by copyright law.

Published by Scorched Feathers
Cleveland, OH
www.scorchedfeathers.com

ISBN: 978-0-578-58234-4
Library of Congress Control Number:2019914718

For all you staples, all you glues and strips of tape…
Everyone who keeps my pieces in place.

SHARDS BY PAGE

20-Something 9

The Answer Is 12

Marks of a Maniac 14

Unknown Numbers 16

Cartoon Sky 18

Enabler 21

Peace in Hand 23

Future's Kiss 26

Believe in Myself 27

This Place Called War 29

Yes 30

Why Do I Live On? 31

Hike In the Early Morning 32

For My Boys (Take Me With You) 33

Woman in the Universe 34

Fingertips 36

My Good-Bye to Willie and Channing 37

Where I Stand 38

The Wee Hours of the First Day of Spring 39

What This Is 41

The Version I Sent Him 45

Books of Hymns 48

I Am Alpha 50

Me to Them 52

I Deserve 53

She Flies 54

A Poem to Myself 56

I Wanna Fuck a Poet 58

Trinkets in a Box 59

Dance 60

Begin Again 61

Stuck In a Tree 62

What Was Him 63

You in My Space 66

Lovely Mirage 67

So, There 68

Sexy Scar 69

Taking the Time 70

Date Purse 71

Residual 72

Intense 74

In a Bit of Love 76

Quiet Alone...77

He Misses 78

Worthless..80

What's Left...81

Where He Used to Sit 82

Tick Tock 83

Gone 84

Easy...85

I Misbehave...86

Kissed By Music (Celebrating Shannon) 87

To Miss...89

Unlovable 90

Our Float..91

How She Steps 92

Start 94

Regret..95

Welcome Home 96

Don't Love Me 97

Our Long Ago 99

Our Now..100

Explicitly	101
At the Dive	102
Warrior	103
Another One About Her	105
Chemistry	106
She Felt That	107
Scars Near My Heart	108
Things I Almost Texted You Last Night	109
Lost Cause	112
Grudge	113
All I Do Is Miss You	114
Powerless	115
The Poet	116
Almost Over You	118
Ticklish Scar	119
The House That Time Built	120
Shards by Title	124
Who She Is	126

20-SOMETHING

There is a place in which we belong:
Valleys race against the echoes
of children laughing their songs.
Ink flows from pens without thought,
or a rhythm or rhyme
or the passing of time…Oops!

There are no boundaries in this chaos,
no rules to keep these soldiers in line;
just a pen writing electro-pulses
sent from my mind
through these eyes
and into these blue-tipped fingers
left over from the twentieth century.

But, the longer I watch this red ink
under my control, from my vein,
the more milliseconds slink by,
the more I need to rhyme and say:

It's all I've ever had in this world!
A book full of implied secrets,
the sand on the beaches,
a story of sneetches,
out of reaches,
speechless.

I'm crawling up from this pen
that replies to me now and then
with some cute giggle of times that are past…
All these words, perhaps my last.

Getting older, but left here floating
at the tip of the water,

full of hate and self-loathing
because I'm already on the 36th line,
but I can't stop the rhyme.

That fat cAT SAT UNTIL I BEAT HIM
WITH THE THICK END OF A STICK
AND WATCHED HIM BLEED;
HE IS DEAD.

Breath…

That's just a lie I've told;
I fed and petted him instead.

My place is not here
in reality's dress,
nor this molded body,
nor the heart in my chest.
So why does it hurt so much now
of all those things then,
of this place, how?

It is my final rebellion
and my last chance to take out the format
that this society insists I follow.
To forget about the meter of words
and to just,
for once,
write what's on my mind;
stop breaking these lines
in prescribed places. To change
colors if I wish;
about order words of forgetting the…
to find my place
somewhere in all this.

I know I have so far left to go
to find a place where I belong.
It never seems to be the place we live;
I realize all the lines
as I seek myself to find
those fat cats cradled
in little girls' arms.

Silence this hurt, this rage;
fall quiet, you tears,
go easy, breath;
Just step.

THE ANSWER IS

I'm experiencing a sadness I've never felt before.
It's a distance that I can't gap if I try.
I wonder why.

I dance around bushes like a 5-year-old,
like the lies I've told;
Like a chant in the schoolyard,
the radio buzzes on and on,
remembering times so long gone,
dreams that have flown.
My child has outgrown my body.

The answer is: I need a way out of it.

The skin needs peeled away,
the bone crushed to pieces,
veins dried to dust.
A silhouette, in the night, emerges:
my soul, my me–the real me–
invisible to anyone who ever mattered.
Gone.
All words shattered
against red brick walls,
paintings of longing, of dreams.
My screams unheard,
no lips to form words;
the pen has run dry, no ink;
what I think is numbed:
no voice, no performance, no applause.

The answer is: I need out of this.
So I pick up my pen
and escape like smoke
from heavy steel cuffs,

a dungeon damsel
locked up and stuff.
Like a peasant girl awaiting her prince:
Been fucked, but I'm still a virgin.
Still waiting for all those adventures,
the dangers,
the fixtures on a marble mantel.
Chandeliers and sconces
reflected in mirrors down a long hall,
sheer white curtains dance,
interrupting the path in this cave.

I feel brave,
I feel free,
like I want to know what's inside of me.
He calls from behind a wooden door
as heavy as a thousand planets,
cracked enough to breathe.

The real answer is
this tiny scream lumped in my throat,
this whimper for fantasy.

MARKS OF A MANIAC

Creep into madness,
knees bent and leaves wet,
a vine slouches on an old couch
to the heh-heh-heh
of the ceiling fan;
silence everywhere else
in this empty room.
Tranced inside the strain,
grunting out tears
for handing over my reins;
Nothing remains
but the two-try
marks of a maniac.

I ain't here,
this ain't real,
but I feel a drop
for each loss:
two cracks in the plaster
and holes where the pictures
once held it together,
kept it from decomposing
like everything else,
like cut stems
with no water to sip,
hurts like the truth
that I can't grow new roots.

Hands open in wait,
numb over the cliff of time,
the breaking of a perfect line
around names carved
in the bark of a tree;
cheesy, but like a nibble

on your nipple.
Open and catching
the trickle of summer mist,
empty fist,
preceded by the
marks of a maniac.

Tug reality's ribbon,
rip the paper to shreds—
That's how I know
there's nothing left.
Heh-heh-heh-heh,
drop my pen
from drying roots,
pick up a sharper blade
for this much pain,
this box full of truth:
a less-than-nothing
glued immobile;
a once-joke vegetable
marked by a maniac.

UNKNOWN NUMBERS

Sirens sing through a cracked window,
echo through the empty crevices
of dusty shelves,
scream to visibly cold grates
behind a door that never opens.
Empty banks already broken and spent
on the way my life went.

Spread-eagle on a used blanket
on a mattress on the floor,
eyes whip open to the ringing.

Wake up lonely for the same thing
for the third time today;
ignore it out of shame,
the ringing back again.
Wake up lonely and there's nothing to give;
nothing but the things that are needed to live.

Two species of plants,
not sure which,
have survived in this air
for at least a year;
one grown from a seed,
a one that has breeded.

Unknown are all my dreams
as time peaks in my mid-twenties;
a dying princess listening to the streets
behind the ringing of the caller I know
by lighted LCD: Unknown Number.

Hanging from bloody wrists
in a shit-hole cold apartment,

miles from home, alone and delirious
from hunger and withdrawal
from cigarettes, unbalanced,
frail to the touch
with nothing much to hang on to.

Things were going to be
so different by now,
before all these reminders
of just how bad some choices were.

For this Unknown reason
I'm ashamed of being 20-something–
phase of conscious stupidity–
having nothing secure
except the ringing.

CARTOON SKY

My breaking day,
yolk on a blue plate,
sloppy and dripping
into highway lines,
making its correction
on my direction.
Trained in bad habits
like rabbits, only worse;
curse because—fuck you!
No one has to explain
themselves to no one,
double-negative answers
sputtered upward
from smokestack factories;
a few pencil scratches
that swerve into the flames
of villains on buildings
against a cartoon sky…

Oh my—
I drift away from the right line,
grind over holes
to keep me awake,
get me to class,
get me to work on time,
keep me driving
to my next destination.
Prescription lens
for textbook squiggly
condensation explanations,
meanings for its
deceiving appearance.
Half-purple waking from black,
blushing hues splash

in fragments
of yesterday's sins.

But they make love;
the pink and blue
fantasy unfolds over road,
over the edge
of reality's cartoon sky.
Makes you wonder why
we can't tell the difference;
educated to expect
endings with stars'
handprints in pavement.
Like, if maybe I'm famous,
or can just make my payments,
my place on the dance floor
of Heaven will be
left open for me;
up where fog is just
a cloud on the ground,
vapored tears spilt from the glass
that toasted this center,
this song,
and reminded me of everything
that's gone.

Retinas inflame
to see the sun tracing
each leaf in the distance;
and, as each nuance
reflects into my eyes
in shades we can't see
in the absence of light,
bouncing from particles
behind this highway painting
of miles and miles to nowhere;

somewhere instinct
makes me pick up speed,
leave this place
at the cartoon-checkered flag,
as I realize I can still win
this cloud-chasing race
on their concrete.

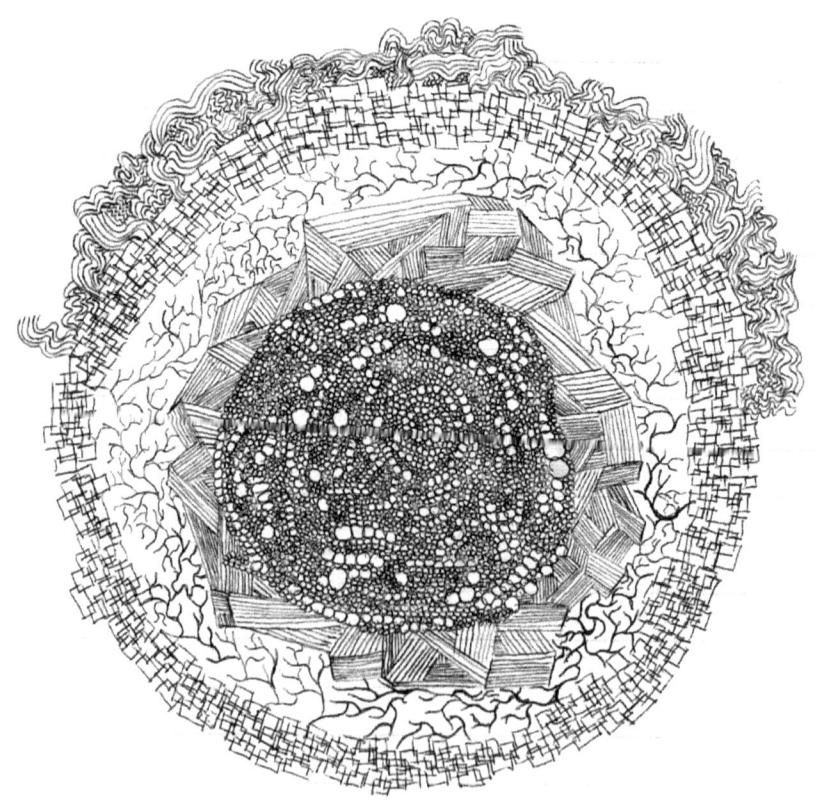

ENABLER

Ah, the weight of a lie
dripping,
    drop,
        drop,
            sigh
because I take
everything I'm getting
    better,
stronger in my jaw
to fake a smile
while I entertain myself
with a button phrase,
watch you enrage
and say exactly what I knew
you'd shift the blame
and say what you said
    Remember when?
Quit listening, drift away,
why can't yesterday
play our song again?
Paper doll model bride,
top of a new matrix
line of reputation;
    erase, fix memories
overwritten when we control
ourselves in a slave.

Ah, the weight of alone
dripping,
    drop,
        drop,
            moan
Ah, masturbate
security in bedding

      wetter,
stronger in my head
protective code
done entertaining myself
with strange gadgets,
save the madness
and do exactly what I do:
I shift the shame
    into a secret
        journal entry.
Quit pretending, come back in,
clean up another mess
of desperate need;
Crumble decayed totem,
god of my sweetest dreams
    tossed in penny wishes,
Repeat, same memories
stepping into this here
    fear of freedom.

PEACE IN HAND

Holding my peace and lighter,
my grip fading, looser,
slowing what I think
so I can hear it,
make sense
and find closure
for everything left open.
Up to dry lips,
inhale bliss,
puff reality
back into perspective:

A moment passing
is just a moment,
even if the world's racing
to catch this or that,
feeling beaten,
cheated out of life and love
with price-tag walls
that repeat
the same old stories
in each of our scenarios.
Alternate pawns,
pieces that move on
no matter how many times
we have fallen.

Like everything,
we have a beginning
and end,
leaving us alone
from time to time.
The half-ash picture
fixes nothing of this hurt

years on down life,
crying in the strangest places,
repainting faces
that once smiled.

Reach out for something–
anything to keep going,
like moaning, love, god, mother.
Wanting someone, anyone
to stop and see
that everyone is disconnected,
spinning inside
discount concoctions,
swallowing whatever is on the spoon,
forgetting we're the same,
like hallowed stone,
empty alone.

Peace in hand–
stop–
and make a little sense
of all the nonsense
that we can hear.
Things wondered:
the commotion of the day
broken like bottles
on the edge of a bar,
cut by swaying, limping,
left-over shards
now in slow motion.
Play along
to the harps of the streets,
because we miss meanings,
doomed to never have answers
to some things.

We'll never know.

But like everything,
we have a beginning
and end,
painting lines
on our own pages
from time to time.
We just have to get
our peace in hand
and puff reality
back into perspective:

We're all just moments passing,
erased before anyone
remembers anything;
victim commercials
of the remote control,
changed and ignored
for better things.
So we can scribble our lines,
defeat the stress
we've been wondering in;
get pretty good
at this thing called life
with our peace in hand,
our moment in time.

FUTURE'S KISS

Splash away the sunset,
oh, just let it melt away,
drip down the canvas
of another passing day.

Time is only future's kiss
running sand into the sea
Liquid splish on the sides of cliffs
setting wishes to fly free.

    Seed births life into being
    echoes itself in the breeze

Dream away sad notions,
smears of second's lipstick,
collar-stained potions
of all yesterday's missed trips.

Life is only today's hand
swiping minutes into hours;
Lesson-chanced bits of sand
kiss seeds to wilted flowers.

    Night splish-splashes forward
    comes day to brush away stars.

BELIEVE IN MYSELF

I don't need any god
To teach me right from wrong;

To make me strong
Or give me a shot,
Or get me out of bed today,
Keep my heart good this way.

Every pulsing equation,
Vibrations of my mind
Evolving over time,
Resolving what I'm dealt,
Yesterday's frustrations.
Thought questions itself,
Has no answers to utter;
I'm not in my mind,
Not my own child;
God must be my mother.

I am created by my mother.

Another study of
Me.

Together; father, reacting with
One who begets me.

Back in the vibration
Everything makes sense,
Lingering consequences;
I'm only a production–
Earth-and-time child,
Very sure this time
Even I will fizzle out.

I don't need any god;
No, I get up and move on.

My strength from nature,
Years of scars overcome;
Scraped knees gone straight.
Every particle of me sure
Life begins and ends; that
Forever lasts only each day.

THIS PLACE CALLED WAR

Ed never cries.
I hear him crying in his bed.
Tomorrow he leaves, his day is near;
His tears, against everything he said
about this place called War,
where women and children, like me,
are saved from monsters.
He stood tall when he told us,
brave as he patted my head
and told me to have trust
in the soldiers to come home again.
…to come home again?

Might he not come home from War?

Ed never cries.
Mom and I are crying for him.
His bag all packed, his day is here,
But Ed looks really scared.
He's not tall and brave anymore; like us,
he's afraid of the monsters.
He picks me up and squeezes,
won't let go of me.
He cries and hugs and holds on tight.
What if I let him go?
If I let him go…

Will he come home from War?

YES

One more shot
breeze under my skirt
forgiven

WHY DO I LIVE ON?

Why do I live on?
Soft lullaby, a song
to my brother fallen,
April morning;
Thought I was stronger
than the sun,
splashing dawn;
hollow sounds, my sobs,
because you're gone…
Why do I live on?

Drawn by Edward Carman, a gift with his letter from some place far away. I miss him every second I live on. That never changes.

HIKE IN THE EARLY MORNING

I stretch out my fingers
    through the tracks of lips;
    that chill softness
dripping and running
    from thumb to something.

Echoed screams on treetops
    bounce through sunray blades;
    stories they sang
bird or wind fiddle,
    love or lust riddle?

Light in the peripherals
    flash and pirouette
    through wind-sliced feathers,
tracing all the leaves
    at nuanced degrees.

I rev up for a sigh;
    Good-bye setting moon,
    the wind's perfume
pours from moist petals:
    earth, twigs and metals.

I gasp open to speak,
    ice stings to the roots,
    pangs of a truce
my tongue tasted sour,
    but heart empowered.

FOR MY BOYS (TAKE ME WITH YOU)

Eye level makes the right connection.
Dream things like no one else dreams them.
Want life.
Another step is all it takes to move on.
Release whatever is dragging you down.
Dance when your feet like the sound.

Wish because it's fun to wish.
Invest when you don't care what you get.
Life's payoff is a million moments.
Listen to every way someone speaks.
Insist on respect and honesty.
Allow your heart to love through fear.
Memories celebrate when lifetimes end.

Create each day on a blank page.
Happiness takes a big dose of self-love.
Anticipate consequences, then choose.
Need people, not things.
Never sit when you should rage.
Imagine every way it could be.
Never get stuck in your sad stories.
Give yourself the strength you need.

Allow yourself to walk away.
Leave the past to your lessons learned.
Expect to get what you've earned.
X–sometimes no words fit your poem.
Allow yourself a new page for a new line.
Need your freedom more than time.
Defend what's you.
Echo things doused in good rhythms.
Remind yourselves every day that I love you.

WOMAN IN THE UNIVERSE

I'm invisible,
vapor,
a motion blur
against laser-sharp winter,
a soft breeze
stinging your cheek numb;
I am a ray of sunlight
in a bright room,
a cell in a fingernail,
shrimp in the ocean,
woman in the universe.
You don't see me,
or you don't like what you see,
but this is as sexy as I get;
yeah, I'm working on this,
and this,
and this,
and deep-down in this.
But, when I'm hands-in-the-air
next to the iPod
and a cheap party light,
swaying and bouncing side to side,
feeling that then
and this here in a song,
when I'm begging you
to say something
before I give up on you…
This is as beautiful as I get,
a notebook
capturing my pen,
but it doesn't make you
want to touch my skin,
doesn't push you off the couch,
doesn't get you on your feet

dancing with me.
I spend these hours
alone
in the next room,
right where I can recognize
in your eyes
that you never really saw me.

FINGERTIPS

We were once a red crack on the horizon,
a moment frozen in that slice of light,
droplets of rain steamed away
in crazy gradients from dark to bright.
If only we could have stayed
any shade that didn't turn blue,
didn't become skin, scorched and torn,
swollen and bruised;
if I didn't need to be more,
feel more
like fingertips warmed
under my dress,
I bet I could just lift my shoulders
and change the subject,
become static like you
only tuned into
alpha waves zipping off the TV.
My numb hands would just open,
let whatever I was hoping for
crash to the floor;
bounce or shatter or
splatter from the scar of our memory.

MY GOOD-BYE TO WILLIE AND CHANNING

I will miss your kisses,
I will miss your smiles,
but I will think of you,
oh, all the time.
If you find yourself lonely
and missing me, too,
close your eyes, cross your arms
and feel me hugging you.

WHERE I STAND

I want you.
We're so in tune, it's wrong,
it's my new favorite song that I can't stop feeling.
Every time it's on, I stop to dance and sing
to your absence noticed by my skin;
I can imagine you,
oh, over and over and over again,
breathing into my hair
every particle of space
we eliminate
inside me.
I'm sorry but you make my heart race,
and I can't see with anything that isn't touching you,
oh, this groove I have to learn from you
as I give to you;
oh, you,
until all I can breathe is your name.

THE WEE HOURS OF THE FIRST DAY OF SPRING

Sometimes I stare at a blank page,
too much to say
to pick a letter to start;
begin anywhere at all,
but tonight I'm six tall drinks
and half a meaningful playlist in;
bent around what he won't say,
but you did.
I'm dancing alone again,
untouched
skin and essence.
I think he's just walked away
this time too many,
and I've given up on him.
Fuck this drink in my left hand
and the pen in the other;
this pipe on the table,
and fuck this song on the iPod
that makes me wonder
why I'm wasting my time,
why I'm settling for distance
in every instance of my love.

Why is everyone so far away?

I have to get out of Cleveland for a few days.

Empty out my heart and head
and figure out where I'm going next,
because I thought I could
give this empty dining room
a thousand more shots;
write down this want enough times

that feeling it could be enough,
but it's not.
I have some lines to add,
a few breaths I need to take,
before I do anything
with this text I've rewritten
too many lines
because I can't find the right shade
for this place I'm shackled to.
I can't hit "send"
because these letters suggest
that you find some way
to let me be your deviance,
let us make the opposite of sense
and eliminate at least one distance.
There's no reason we should settle
for not being seen
nor understood
nor felt all the way through.
Hey, it's not you;
and it's definitely not me;
this is just what we
happen to be.

WHAT THIS IS

I want you with insanity,
with every particle of space I am,
every wicked little wanting I come to be
in what we're both imagining:
the edge of a desk
in an empty office,
heavy breath,
soaking wet,
teeth;
my god, you taste like coffee,
and I take your want for me,
twist it to this depth,
oh, drowning in those lips,
drowning you in these hips.

I'm chest-deep into what this is,
another splinter in the crack
burning through my essence in there;
right there–the spicy sting
that tells me it will never go back
to a metered beating;
It's unpredictable and unslow,
nowhere left to go
but any place unknown,
and now there will always be a trace
of what this is,
oh, what it is.

I know when I'm a mountain,
and when I'm a grain of sand.
And, right now, I can barely stand.

I need a while,
just give me a few days

to pace this into sense,
to figure out another way
to keep our line drawn,
to stop singing these songs in my head
every time I see your eyes;
See, I'm just too deprived in my other life,
I don't know whether I should hold on
or fly;
so many whys and what-ifs,
oh, what it would do to the kids.

Maybe I'm greedy,
so fucking needy I may never be complete;
Shouldn't I feel pretty lucky
to have everything I do;
what some others never get,
never even get close to?
A front porch looking in,
little arms choke-hugging me
at the end of a day's accomplishments;
food in our stomachs,
a clean bathroom and kitchen,
cars that get us to our destinations;
because I've had so much less than this,
before I gave everything to make this
into what it is.
oh, what it is.

Look at what I give,
what I gave every–oh, every day:
words of affirmation,
physical attention,
quality time and conversation,
always at his service,
never holding back gifts;
and all the telling of what I need and want,

oh, over and over and over again,
and now that I'm looking at the present
all I can think of is
everything this isn't,
oh, what it isn't.

If all we ever achieve in life is living,
a little bit of time
to find out how good it can get,
damn it, I am missing it;
because all I'm doing is half-living,
one foot brushing
against the safe side of the line
and the other nowhere near touching
anything but dead grass,
letting excuses pass
so I can believe it's enough;
so that I can keep forgiving
that he wouldn't answer these wants
until my hand was pushing the door open,
until he became no longer what I want.
He is not what I am.
oh, who I am.

An animal pure-bred to slither,
rub my belly through the dirt of this decision;
please be the good that I won't be,
the mountain to my speck–
Me, this grain–
until I can refocus the line of my wanting;
because it needs to be my wind
that blows the door open,
and I can't get you off that desk…
you still make my heart race
and then I can't breathe…
I have no…

I want you in this insanity,
but don't want to lose you to it.

This is what it is,
and, oh, what it is.

THE VERSION I SENT HIM

I know when I'm a mountain,
and when I'm a grain of sand.
And, right now, I can barely stand.

I need a while,
just give me a few days
to pace this into sense,
to figure out another way
to keep our line drawn,
I'm just too deprived in our life,
I don't know whether I should hold on
or fly;
so many whys and what-ifs,
oh, what it would do to the kids.

Maybe I'm greedy,
so fucking needy I may never be complete;
Shouldn't I feel pretty lucky
to have everything we do;
what some others never get,
never even get close to?
A front porch looking in,
little arms choke-hugging me
at the end of a day's accomplishments;
food in our stomachs,
a clean bathroom and kitchen,
cars that get us to our destinations;
because I've had so much less than this,
before I gave everything to make this
into what it is.
oh, what it is.

Look at what I tried to give,
what I gave every–oh, every day:

words of affirmation,
physical attention,
quality time and conversation,
always at your service,
never holding back gifts;
and all the telling of what I need and want,
oh, over and over and over again,
and now that I'm looking at the present
all I can think of is
everything this isn't,
oh, what it isn't.

If all we ever achieve in life is living,
a little bit of time
to find out how good it can get,
damn it, I am missing it;
because all I'm doing is half-living,
one foot brushing
against the safe side of the line
and the other nowhere near touching
anything but dead grass,
letting excuses pass
so I can believe it's enough;
so that I can keep forgiving
that you wouldn't answer these wants
until my hand was pushing the door open,
until you became no longer what I want.
You are not what I am.
oh, who I am.

An animal pure-bred to slither,
rub my belly through the dirt of this decision;
Me, this grain–
until I can refocus the line of my wanting;
because my wind is blowing the door open,
I no longer feel for what this is…

and I want to leave…
I have no…

I want your happiness,
but I won't lose me to it.

This is what it is,
and, oh, what it is.

BOOKS OF HYMNS

I feel like I'm an open book
whose pages like to be flipped,
sniffed and ripped a little deeper
in careless fits of reading;
And you're covered in dust
because you're so afraid
I might not like what you say
or who you've become.
I say, "Fuck it, let's throw down
and find some way to get it on,"
But I'm aware
we'll each drown as one,
because you'll be scared
and I need to sing my song.
I might be totally wrong
but if I'm going to spend faith
on something to make me stronger,
to make me feel every sting
through this needy skin,
make me want to breathe,
I'm going to sing about
the fingers that push my pages
over, up and through my story,
in the chair,
on the table,
across the phone,
in words in stone,
imaginable,
deep down in there,
Because it feels good in here.
But you don't read poetry,
don't feel these tunes the way I do,
and you won't dance,
take a chance,

expand
or fly
or wonder why
or scream
or chase dreams
or sing
or do any of these things
with me.
And I just want to leave–
let you be afraid
and let me sing my praises
to the breeze
of my cover slamming shut,
blowing away your dust
as you mumble a verse
under your breath,
but it doesn't inflate my balloon
of happiness,
and I don't know if your prayers
can clean up this mess.

I AM ALPHA

They tell me I am alpha,
the kind of woman
who wants a man
to bend me over something
by a fistful of my hair.
I won't deny the truth in there
and how I already play like that,
how I let other alphas
twist my arm behind my back
while I rile them with jabs,
my bad jokes
and ball-bustin'.

And they are, none of them,
jaw-dropped when I call them
back to bed
because I'm not done yet;
because three cracked bones
and a few bite marks
didn't make me feel enough.
No man wants a woman that tough
long-term.
I make me alone.

They tell me I am alpha,
the kind of woman
who makes me alone
as soon as they step up to me.
I push them hard to watch them fall
to see which ones
bounce back to me
and in how many pieces,
and which ones bounce back
and get even.

Welcome to the alpha club,
they tell;
I am not unique
in what I'm missing,
but I am unique in my honesty.

Well…

I am alpha,
and so I tell them
exactly who I am:
dichotomy--
everything and nothing;
seeker of a sweeter scream,
someone to acknowledge
me for me;
look me in the eyes
and take me on that deep;
but this twisted arm
is the best I'll ever achieve,
because none of them
ever see me
beyond what I seem.

I am alpha,
exiting;
making me alone,
so that they will
finally see me
in what they let go.

ME TO THEM

Sharp on my edgy side
Seriously too honest
Sexy in the eyes
Alpha breed
Caring to scary
Pretty to look at
Driven to dream
Feeling everything
Unique in how I see
Hard to match
Brave to overthink
And take what I need
Quitter
The one who's leaving
Tough lady
Too fast to breathe
Good at what I overdo
Rationally emotional
A good deal
But I worship love
All in when I go in
Pray for sin
Guilty of everything
Lucky to be me
A regarded opinion
Crazy brave to go
Comfortable alone
Gone
But I get weak
Woman

I DESERVE

I deserve someone
who scrapes his knees
on the long way down
to make me feel wanted,
and loved,
and desired.
I deserve someone
who will nearly drown
in his flesh haunted
to touch me;
just fucking touch me
like he wants me.

He, who will design wings
to eliminate any space;
to be with me
even when he can't be with me.
I deserve someone
who admires the shades
and the strokes
as I paint him in my life;
who takes that brush
and isn't afraid to sing me,
dance me,
make me believe us
every time his lips spark mine.

SHE FLIES

If you could bundle
the sunrise forgotten,
the one you see
on the other side
of all night long,
wide awake,
and then never the same;
a breath pulled through teeth
and then released with his name;
twist it through an ink pen
into shapes,
symbols,
into a period on the page;
she is my essence,
the subject of the sentence:
a stupid, euphoric girl
peaked at both ends of the spectrum.
wanting some,
and then more,
and open wider than ever before.
More she than I've ever been.
Swimming as fast as I swim;
giving every saltwater breath
this body has to give
to let her live.
And I may not make her end,
not with how waist-deep I am
in the madness her wave is:
splitting the seeds,
the trees,
the things she thought we could be;
the fear of horizons
we'll never approach,
never feel against her skin;

leaving behind,
letting go,
her fear of never finding
anything as meaningful
as my heart needs.
She'll uncurl my fingers
and watch our ashes disintegrate,
melt into the exhale
of his hand waving
good-bye,
but she won't cry.
She flies.

A POEM TO MYSELF

I am no Hercules,
my knees are raw,
bleeding from scabs
imprinted by the sand
baked into the substrate
scraping the skin
from my hands dragging
in my crawling on
because I'm numb through them;
I can't feel anything
through this everything,
so I'm freeing the parts of me
that he left thin,
see-through,
invisible,
miserable.

I am a willful walking away
when love doesn't go my way,
when he won't say
what I want him to say,
when he won't introduce
his fingers to my deviance,
knock out my wind,
give in,
sin,
I go ahead and quit again.

I'm no stronger
than my happiness,
ashes pumping through
the screeching ringing
between the chambers
that regulate the must-haves

to the needs,
to the fantasy and dream,
to the ears absorbing my meanings
and the ones who believe
I need nothing or no one
to be me,
and I disagree with them,
tell them I still need someone
on the receiving end
of my abundances,
the flames that flick
and singe everything to stiff edges.

Then they remind me
that I make the best of being alone:
In the middle of the madness,
the empty,
the dark place
most people run from,
I make it my own happy moment:
I sit down and write a poem
for me.

I WANNA FUCK A POET

Someday someone
is going to feel like
this crazy
is the most beautiful thing
he's ever seen
and contribute a few lines
to commemorate
the good feeling
he had for me.

TRINKETS IN A BOX

The quiet
carries the weight
of everything:
all the spaces
carved to shapes
of things
we use for remembering.

DANCE

Life
is a bunch of people
coming and going,
hiding and showing.
It's all about knowing
    to sway,
        to slide,
            to step,
    swing,
switch to the beats
of every moment
    anyway.

BEGIN AGAIN

The shades
disintegrate into gradients,
a purple searing
the spotted darkness,
a bruising that alights
a quick slice through its skin,
the cover ablaze,
too bright,
and then dull
and blowing away,
a singed page awaits
how the next moment
begins.

STUCK IN A TREE

Handle of a plastic bag
tangled in barren Autumn branches
that used to be green
and spotted with pink petals;
the ghost lifted,
shifted and dipped,
rested against an empty nest,
and then flipped away,
bounced any way
opposite the quiet,
pulled,
opened to catch
a bigger breeze,
but only a breaking
of plastic
or tree…

WHAT WAS HIM

Every day at 4:17…

I remember what was him:
We lay on the floor in front of the TV,
eyes half closed, unblinking
while we master Dragon Warrior
on the first Nintendo console;
wrestling on Saturday mornings,
covering holes in the wall
with old hair-band posters;
throw-down brawls in the living room
when we were latch-key
and free to become whatever the streets
had in mind for our stories.

I won't tell mom if you won't.

Every day at 4:17…

I remember what was him:
The only thing connected to me
in the chaos we had no choice in:
the distant lights like warp-speed stars
along the late-night highway,
our faces inches apart
on the backseat heap
of garbage bags of things
we actually had to take with us.
Whatever bed, whatever floor,
wherever was next,
together,
we just had to keep moving forward
until we found more,
made things better than this.

We'll be okay.

Every day at 4:17…

I remember what was him:
In the outfield on the opposing team
catching my fly at his backside,
four dance steps smashing my pride;
running away with other boys,
quick evading me
so they could sneak magazines;
but then he clapped the loudest
when I hit the homerun mark on the wall;
came back and picked me up
when I slipped on the gravel
and fell trying to catch them all;
and when the boys were gone,
he showed me his collection
of naked women.

Just don't tell mom.

Every day at 4:17…

I remember what was him:
On the other end of the phone
waiting to leave,
reminding me that he was him
and there was no need for worrying;
out of reach and not knowing
if the news reports were about him
or someone else's "him";
then getting that call mid-morning,
and then watching the clock on the wall
for weeks,

waiting for my "him" returned in pieces;
letting him bury some of our history,
but keeping the rest with me.

I won't let you go.

Every day at 4:17…

YOU IN MY SPACE

You in my space
feels a little breath held
static in my bones
warm as a candle wick
blanket pulled to chin
and I am in,
again.

LOVELY MIRAGE

He tells me
the color of the clouds
is a mirage;
that the pink,
the purple,
the blues,
and silver lining
are just sloppy light
bouncing
off water particles.
He tells me
the love that I want,
that I need
sleeps among the billows,
the moisture
turned raindrop,
but, unlike him,
my heart doesn't
settle for what my eyes see.

SO, THERE

No one will ever love you
like I burn all the tracks
of all the tears
that evaporate midair,
just in time
before you care
too much about me.
You are meant to be
exactly how much you are
not
here.
So, there.

SEXY SCAR

You are a deep puncture,
a wound
beyond the possibility of suture,
scabbed to a ticklish
missing-you scar,
a decoration
that gives my heart
a little character,
a little humor
and armor
that other hearts
seem to find irresistible,
and so it becomes too easy
to be without you.

TAKING THE TIME

Watch me run away
to the steamy bath
and candles
and Bukowski thoughts
and ice cubes melting
in the slippery glass
and nepenthe
I alight in its intensity
let it burn
right through everything
that insists
on being felt in me,
dissipate when I finally
exhale,
let it go
like steam
like smoke
like memory words
I will reread
until I accept
that the feeling is all
that it meant.

DATE PURSE

House key,
I.D. and ATM card,
small wad of cash to spend
in a pocket separate
from my lip balm,
cherry.

Toothbrush.
Toothpaste.
Eye paste.
Macgyver-like folding brush.
The things I need
to recreate
the illusion of me
come morning.

A tight squeeze
for my phone
to let my girls know
where I'm going.

Condoms –
Regular and Magnum,
because you don't want to
have to forego
should a cock grow
Magnum-size.

Hand sanitizer.

RESIDUAL

Dust-like mud in the crevices,
staining the wall around frames,
in them, we are frozen
with a couple smiles
that made me think
we played the same thud
against our rib cages.

Now I see it's feigned.

When I sang,
you didn't pause for the tune,
twist the keys,
open your room…
you hated my poems,
never wanted to swing hips
to my bass thump,
not one;
never loved who I was.

Since you are
where I began
exactly who I am,
I'll never trust anyone
to stay.

That's why I run away,
hide the ashes,
I crushed up
those old photographs,
stuffed their dust
where boards meet,
into corners
in back of cabinets,

into cracks under rugs,
into the pores
of porcelain tubs.

Go on and scrub…

It just turns to mud
in the crevices,
stains on the wall around frames…

INTENSE

Here, love,
take these few lines
that explain why I'm afraid
of your intense
erosions of my solid rock,
and then I'll let you
break me into grains,
static scattered
over the expanse,
dented by fingers into symbols,
love letters
that scribble the beach
as far as anyone can see.

And, on the heels
of our footprints,
those letters like trenches,
inverted scabs of scratches,
histories of our hearts
we abandon
to erase in the waves.

That's the thing:
We forget the sting,
the squealing birds,
the screeching,
all the while swallowing
fish alive.
We deny,
tell ourselves lies.

Pretend we hear them sing:
It's just a tune
that's new.

We just need a new shimmy,
a shoe whose heels won't sink
in the sand,
and then we could be
everything,
we can.

Oh, this
is
going to sting.

But we try,
because
we need it–that's why.

Like we needed all of those
prints in the dunes
to dry,
to forget,
to make us thirsty,
erode us enough
to tolerate the chaos
that craves us,
so that you would crash
this intense moment,
chip it right off the cliff
and scratch it into my skin;
and so I would empty my pen
on this page
for you.

IN A BIT OF LOVE

I will always love him
Even though he doesn't deserve me
One bit.

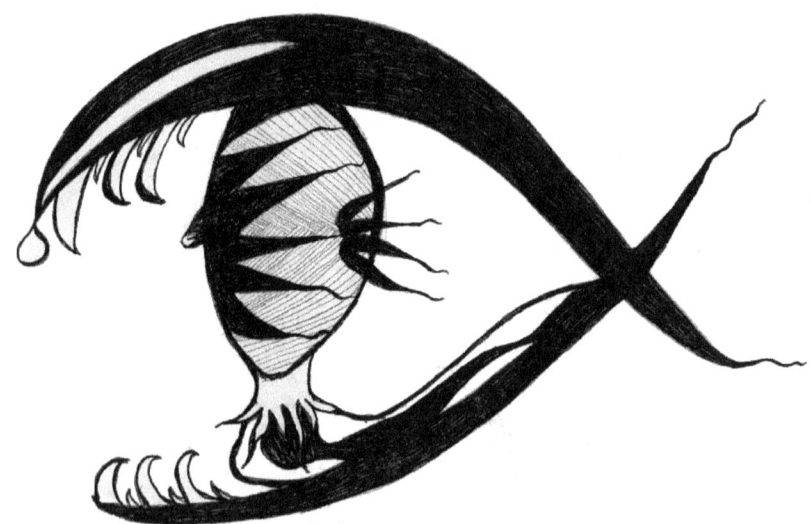

QUIET ALONE

Today I am stone,
Gray with flecks of sand,
shiny at the bone.

I've forgotten none,
They all cross my mind,
Come back to their home

As soon as I'm alone,
I scrub at the stains
Of everyone who's gone.

HE MISSES

He never undresses me.

So I check my skin,
the dimples,
the divots,
the extra bit
and shapes it spins
from all angles:

>   Mirror, mirror on the wall
>   am I beautiful at all?

I see me,
imperfect;
it's who I'd rather be.
There are stories,
intentional scars
from all the times
I knew I'd trip and fall
and scrape my knee,
bust my lip,
crack my skull,
stretch my skin,
lose a brawl,
but still went and did it all;
these are the memories
of everyone
I need to recall
once in awhile.

And isn't this reflection
Pretty?
Sexy?
Something that attracts fingers?

I let my own linger
in all the right places
at the right pressure
for the right time,
perfect motion
over each warm tissue
over and over and…
until I need nothing
from him.

    Mirror, mirror on the wall
    am I strong?

Then, why do I care
whether he undresses me?

WORTHLESS

my heart is broken,
which means my skin
and everything within
is worthless.

WHAT'S LEFT

Returned everything
but this t-shirt
so big
it barely touches
my skin.
Oh, in it
I am still next to you,
and we are cool
like a Spring morning
near some pond
in some woods
near your house;
we are scorching
like my thigh sliding
over your thighs,
and my lips
closing inches,
breath witness
to some ghost
of warmth
in your eyes.

I remember.

WHERE HE USED TO SIT

He's an assprint
in your cushion.
Time will inflate you
back to your original shape.

TICK TOCK

Because every second
is another chance
another chance
another chance
another chance
another chance
another chance
another precious moment
to begin again.

Stand.

Run.

GONE

He has become
just a memory
tucked inside
the melodies
of 23 songs.

I sing him
to leave him
gone.

EASY

I'll never be easy,
and if I seemed it
that's because I felt you,
oh, the spark of us,
in me
through me
with me
before your fingers
ever touched my skin.

I MISBEHAVE

Behave.
Because it won't be easy
untangling your hands
from my hair
if they find their way there,
squirming them
away from my neck and back,
away from how you feel
this deep in here,
oh, that way,
right here.

I won't say "no" to wherever
this feeling throws us;
we can't go slow
and we can't help but go there;
I know us.
So, if you feel even a touch
that we shouldn't,
then maybe we shouldn't
even show.

But, oh, love,
if you want to see
how tangled we can be
everywhere we are thrown,
come here,
get free,
and let your heart
misbehave
with me;
oh, this way,
right there.

KISSED BY MUSIC (CELEBRATING SHANNON)

You are mine to remember.

The icy pool
we abandoned
for the hot bathtub
in the hotel room;
our Voodoo Juice
by the big-ounce
styrofoam cup
on the edge of the tub.

This is what I love
about us.

Boomerang,
who really did come back
whenever we called
for our next away.

King David,
his dirty joke
about watering dirt,
halfway on his personal tour
away from the lights,
the music,
and, me, uneasy
that our feet beat opposite
the heartbeats,
and, I meant it,
we were not going into his house for anything!

You know I was right.

And your gift of him…
I know you're supposed to
leave it
in New Orleans,
but then,
no one has ever
called out my need
more completely
than you did when
you made him notice me;
and he…
his intensity…
would, then, let me go
so that all I will ever know
are his marshmallow kisses
everywhere he kissed,
his tattoos and ghetto speak,
short mohawk,
the eyes of his beast
over and over and over again–
Damn, I loved New Orleans–
he is mine to remember,
make immortal
in my memories with you, sister.

We were sunrises
looking for skies
to color with our tune,
and we arose
to precious moments
thundering in our motions;
yes, this is what we do
and what I love
about you.

TO MISS

Yesterday, I heard a song
that crashed
into your piece of me that
I thought I trapped so strong,
so long in my center.
It cried for escape,
to hang onto your space
whether it's wrong,
but you're no longer
in my way,
so I sang our song to your absence
oh, over and over and over again.

Oh, I miss…

UNLOVABLE

That numb
that came from
her bruising my surface,
charring my depth,
that makes it impossible
to trust anyone,
or to grab on
and connect my essence
even for a minute,
and so it drags me
by a fistful of hair
on bleeding knees,
wanting–
no, begging
for all of them
to shove me
away from anything
that might burn
or sting
or slice off a piece
to steal and take
when they run,
escape
unlovable me.

OUR FLOAT

I only have so much air
to blow into our balloon
before it shrivels
into a useless vessel
that will flop down
to splatter the ground
we'll break with our end.

If you want to float away
to the places we named
in those
alone-together moments,
you're going to need
to return your lips
to our kiss
and share your breath.

HOW SHE STEPS

She is dancing around flames,
chanting the most blessed phrases
to some place among the embers,
deep in the ice red stones,
to the black bone she makes into pen,
charred, smoking sticks
scraping a blank page;
she was her once
before you came…

so she'll sway and skip,
slide to kick up dust
to smother all that sin,
she digs her heels in
and grinds that dirt
into recognizable bits
of the lust and love
she once was
before you did
what you did…

with a few spins and turns,
she uncurses the rain,
her hands reaching up and out
to cross the flame
and back in to cross her chest;
she keeps the drops
from staining her cheeks,
from drenching her hair
and sticking strands to her face,
she starts swinging,
jabs and uppercuts,
wild unscreamed screams
targeting the ash burned free

to splatter open space,
her feet pound hard
on the ground
until she can't breathe,
until every memory of your hands
on her skin
is ablaze,
and then dust-like blowing away
like you were just a dream,
because she won't let you
shame
her.

You will not
make
her
weak.

START

Yes.
Let me have you
right like the breath
fleeing your lips,
right like whatever this—
this madness is;
you, whatever you are.
Let me take you
wherever
however far
you've been hiding,
dying in that heart.
Open for me.
Say yes.

REGRET

You lied me
into your madness,
the fucking mess
you didn't confess
until I was completely
undressed,
your fingers pressing
sweet promises
deep, deeper yet
into my mind,
heart and essence,
abusing my openness
with your fantasy trips,
our fantasy arguments
over who of us gets
to cut the grass.
Let me guess:
You're sorry.

Yeah, well,
I was serious.

WELCOME HOME

You know me:
I don't love
just a little bit.
My heart doesn't know
that quantity,
it does not shrink
that tiny.
That's why I stand
warrior
at the door,
why so few get through
anything more
than a few skin-deep layers
of splinters,
grains of the dust
of my wood
that runs full-on
four decades deep.
But, you,
you come the fuck in.

DON'T LOVE ME

Don't like me.
I'm difficult.
I'm strange.
Way a bunch crazy.
I play rockstar
in the rain,
in the living room
in the wee hours of morning,
and again
at three minutes past noon
to some tunes on repeat,
watch me sing
every syllable
of lyric
like there's me in it.

Don't want me.
We will ignite
like flint and steel,
start fires
whenever we connect
at the chest
and everywhere else;
yes, you will need to be
a man strong enough
to melt,
or burn to ash
to float away
on the dust of smoke;
go deep, go shallow;
hang on or let go;
burn down, regrow.

Don't need me.
I'm not whoever
she was.
I will never fill
the empty she left.
I don't have the breaths
to waste
on what-might-have-beens;
life has
so little time to be lived,
and I have so little patience
for anyone
who can't go all in,
because I need
to be intense
deep
unreal
for real
and every chip in
like it has never been
risked before.

OUR LONG AGO

We used to fly these roads
with our eyes closed;
all the hills and the bends
of our moments
we'll race and win
never again;
the 'once upon' untold,
erased,
pages and photographs
sucked out the window,
and our songs on the radio,
my foot on the dash,
and your sweatshirt,
your scent,
all burning black scars
onto the pavement,
warp-speed splashes,
peripheral blurs
of what's not left;
what was me,
who she was,
and how she
would only go
anywhere you'd go—

speed
screech
burn
dirt
haunting
like dust blown,
like smoke—
our long ago.

OUR NOW

What we have
is torturous space,
slices of minutes
when our eyes chase
the other
deep into our hearts,
dreaming
of the right phrase,
the thing to say
to spark and burn down
the rest of these moments
wherein
we are not skin to skin,
your temple to mine,
our breath,
our giving in
to whatever whim
and whenever
we want
for the other.

But we look away.

EXPLICITLY

Say it to me, he says
into my chest-deep breaths…
I might drown him,
but I'm drowning
so I says:

You fulfill my every need,
physically,
emotionally,
whatever my fantasy;
You are magic to me,
a sparkling dizzy
shaken with intensity.
I am vulnerable to you,
I am yours,
I have connected my essence
to anything you are
and were
and will every new day become.
You are my happiness.
I want us.
I am now us.

Then, say it to me,
he says,
simplify
our complexity.
And so I says
into his chest-deep breaths:

I love you.

AT THE DIVE

I just came for the jukebox,
And to write a poem
In the back of this room
While doing shots
Because it's how I forget
What we got--
I mean, what we had,
What we couldn't make last.

WARRIOR

I am the most damaged thing
you've ever seen
this taped and glued
back together.
I've had just about everything
severed and shattered,
stomped on and beaten down
like none of me mattered,
not once,
but, oh,
too many times.

Still, at every new day,
I force my hands open,
stretch these aching fingers
straight,
push them out hard
to scoop in the shards
of who I was
in all my hopes,
when life was…
what it was
that I can't even speak of…

I lift my bleeding cheek
from the pavement,
kneel there,
short grunts to the pain
while I realign,
position my big pieces
and swish my palms
as wide as they'll slide
to collect even the dust of me,
the crumbs

that I paste
into these crevices
with my own blood
and salted rain.

Then, I stand,
and step into my day,
screaming at the seams,
but unable
to unhope.

ANOTHER ONE ABOUT HER

I don't have a word
to name this feel.
Waiting?
Numb?
Undone?
Rage unable to speak?
Forgotten by someone
my heart cannot unlove?

Oh, she's almost gone.
I mean moments.
Days.
Weeks.
Oh, years ago.

Tomorrow?

Never.

I never get to unfeel
her.

CHEMISTRY

What is it about *you*
right now
that makes me write
this moan
that sings like your name,
looks like your face
when I must kiss you,
splashes through me
like your hands,
one on the back of my neck
and the other pinning my arms
to the curve of my back
and pulling me
into you?
Oh, why do I need *you*
right now?

SHE FELT THAT

I'd rather bleed
and know
than never
leave
the pillow.

SCARS NEAR MY HEART

I'm emotional on purpose;
I feel all of my wounds
and, sometimes, they break open
and bleed again
and, sometimes,
something cuts me
right over top of those
synthetic seams
that are way too deep
to heal anymore completely.
Sometimes,
you'll just have to taste
my bleeding
if you want your legend
clawed into my skin
near the key to everything
I will ever be.

THINGS I ALMOST TEXTED YOU LAST NIGHT

I feel the thought of you
everywhere.

Love matters, and you love me.
I love you, so let's just be.
Let's just see, oh, I love you.
You love me, and love matters.

You are attracted
to my faults
as I am
magnetic to yours,
so there's no saving
you or me or us
from the madness
of each other.

If I'm wrong about you,
I just have to be wrong.

I made three glasses
of toasts to your memory,
one for every sip,
every gulp,
every dangling drop
from the rim to my lip,
all the spins and twists
of you,
of what this is…
Five…
Seven…
Uh-oh.

Why does the villain
in my chest
keep loving
your poisonous scent?
Because we still have
open business,
things to say to each other,
things to put in
and pull right back out;
a few more times
to undress
and let us
be dangerous.

I like the way wanting you
tingles my lips,
crawls over my skin,
and makes me pull air
through every seam
that is me
barely threaded together.
I feel the thought of you
everywhere.

But you crushed to dust
the boulder of love
I put in your hands.
Why would I gift you
even another speck
of who I am?

I would have to hate myself
to let you back in.

I regret all the places
you touched me
under my skin.

What we could have been…

One day we'll smile
at each other
again.
One day.
I'm not ready yet.

LOST CAUSE

Your love,
sharp across my wrists,
deep and screaming,
and painfully pleasing;
but never succeeding
in digging out
the necrotic pieces
your poison
stole from me.

GRUDGE

I feed this craving
the ache I've been saving
in the cracked glass jar
of my heart.
Pull out and loop the reruns
of your biggest sins
because I need to keep space,
not fall apart,
not again;
patch me up with anger, hating
everything you are
so I won't let you back in.

ALL I DO IS MISS YOU

All I do is miss you,
feel your absence
in all these tick-tocks,
all these songs of us
all shuffling on repeat,
a parade of thunder
from my thousand
weeping heart beats—

miss you, miss you, miss you—

drenched in the madness
my breaking muscle spends
begging for your presence…

in all this pain
we lovely stained
with all our regrets,
all the bad ways
we went,
all the rain,
what you said
all shuffling on repeat…

breathing the hush
at our song's end,
rewind it again;
I sing us,
and then
all I do is miss you.

POWERLESS

I'm a fuse that trips
when it attempts
to connect to anyone.
I know I run;
I overheat and spark
right before I retreat,
pull my love
way back down deep
into the dark
to hide from the things
I can still feel singed
by everything about him,
and what she did,
and him,
and how I miss
every one of them.
I'm a cable of frayed wires,
a beating pile of scars
in different stages of healing,
tender burns and ticklish moans
depending on
how hard you press them.
I'm all shorted circuits
through everywhere in here,
oh, inside every bit
of everything we ever
might have been
if I weren't so
fried at the switch.

THE POET

I'm a poet,
not meant to be known
until I die,
and that's just fine
by me
because seeing
the dark of your eyes,
those crooked smiles,
the lights and
the quiet and
the heat…
give me anxiety.

Damn it,
I *have* to make sense
of everything that happens:
the loves and
the tragedies;
the sad,
the mad
catastrophes of living
with feelings
painted in shades of words
and rhythms we each
think we hear
in the other.

Because you're there
and I'm here
and this is all kind of personal;
I'm just not sure
whether we're better
together

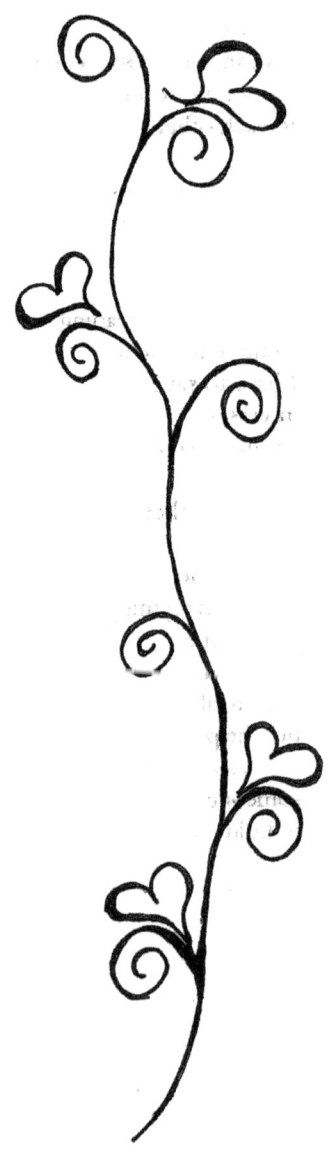

or separate…
Whether we're destined
or cursed.
I mean, what's the worst
thing we've ever done
to each other?

I can only love us
from the distance
of not knowing
any of what it is
that keeps you reading
all these moments
I have to save
in verses
for the two of us.

Being together means:
the poet,
she is alone;
there is everything
but no one.
And, you,
you are alone, too,
but the poet,
she is something,
someone
to hold you.

ALMOST OVER YOU

Just a streak of you
left on my window,
a smudge,
a smear of reddish grey
from my dirty rag,
a stubborn dull splash
of grime ingrained,
surviving the scrub
and my vinegar spritz,
the hard breaths
and quick whips
one side to the other,
across and around
and up and down
via u-turns and figure-eights,
fingernail scrapes
and finger-knuckle rubs;
now, you're just a streak
across my window,
still staining the sun
with your shadow,
so I give us
another spray,
scrape,
rub.

TICKLISH SCAR

A poet doesn't just
love you for a moment.
She lets you puncture her skin
with the way you feel,
lets it heal,
and then rubs it
now and then
to feel you again.

THE HOUSE THAT TIME BUILT

Home is where I've been,
where I am,
and where I'm going.

It is a web of pavement,
winding tar,
trees and houses and bars,
coasting to the car's
low and high bends,
the swinging right,
and left swing,
the speed,
the weed,
the stories
clashing now with then.

Home is crumbled brick
the city demolished years ago–
but I didn't know it,
didn't get that text–
the inverted field of grass
left behind a chain-link fence
that's missing poles,
and subsequently rolled in folds,
twisted, cold, and bent.

It's a bunch of windows
with dark holes
where some kid used to live,
and that kid and that kid;
where we used to speak secrets,
drain a keg to the music,
kiss…
where we spent a few good,

a few bad
syllables of so many moments.

Home is where I'm from,
where I am,
and where I'm going.

I've been gone so long,
just gone,
all these years I was just
moving on and on;
keepin' on keepin' on
like I am stronger
than whatever's going on,
like there is some place
on this rock in space
where I belong.

Home is my brother's tombstone,
the cage my heart must return to
over and over and over again
because there is no end
to this sentence,
and I will serve my time
graveside,
the rest of my life accountable
for how much I loved him;
some roots are too deep
to die.

It's the hum and clack
of metal-grinding trains
on railroad tracks,
always within blocks of my bed
so that I can dream;
so that I can breathe through

and be numb to
the screech,
the whistle,
the beginning,
the sides of
who I'm from.

I am now closer
to the pillow at my end,
my silence,
someone weeping to my absence,
to the memories
I wrote down for them;
a few people
will think of me now and then.
I hope.

Home is where I'm from,
where I am,
and where I'm going.

SHARDS BY TITLE

2

20-Something 9

A

All I Do Is Miss You 114
Almost Over You..............................118
Another One About Her 105
Answer Is, The 12
At the Dive.......................................102

B

Begin Again.......................................61
Believe in Myself 27
Books of Hymns................................48

C

Cartoon Sky 18
Chemistry 106

D

Dance..60
Date Purse 71
Don't Love Me 97

E

Easy 85
Enabler 21
Explicitly 101

F

Fingertips..36
For My Boys (Take Me With You)......33
Future's Kiss......................................26

G

Gone 84
Grudge 113

H

He Misses 78
Hike in the Early Morning.................32
How She Steps..................................92

I

I Am Alpha 50
I Deserve...53
I Misbehave 86
In a Bit of Love 76
Intense..74

K

Kissed by Music (Celebrating Shannon)
....87

L

Lost Cause.......................................112
Lovely Mirage 67

M

Marks of a Maniac 14
Me to Them 52
My Good-bye to Willie and Channing 37

O

Our Float...91
Our Long Ago....................................99
Our Now 100

P

Peace in Hand 23
Poem to Myself, A 56
Poet, The 116
Powerless 115

Q

Quiet Alone 77

R

Regret 95
Residual 72

S

Scars Near My Heart 108
Sexy Scar 69
She Felt That 107
She Flies 54
So, There 68
Start 94
Stuck in a Tree 62

T

Taking the Time 70
The House That Time Built 120
The Version I Sent Him 45
Things I Almost Texted You Last Night 109
This Place Called War 29
Tick Tock 83
Ticklish Scar 119
To Miss 89
Trinkets in a Box 59

U

Unknown Numbers 16
Unlovable 90

W

Warrior 103
Wee Hours of the First Day of Spring, The 39
Welcome Home 96
What This Is 41
What Was Him 63
What's Left 81
Where He Used to Sit 82
Where I Stand 38
Who She Is 126
Why Do I Live On? 31
Woman in the Universe 34
Worthless 80

Y

Yes 30
You in My Space 66

WHO SHE IS

Dude. I say "dude" for lots of meanings. I swear a lot, too, and sometimes experience myself in the third person. I fondle the edge of my right ear when I'm thinking or relaxing or really into what you're saying. This ear caress is a comfort remnant from my childhood that I refuse to outgrow because it was once the only way I felt good. I have been taping pages of hand-written stories and poems together for as long as I can remember. Yet, even as you hold the pages of my first, official book, being a mom is the greatest thing I've ever done on every level of my existence. It's humbling, but empowering. I love two awesome people who started inside my body, and we are learning life together. I like cheap, colorful party lights and have them in almost every room of my house. The way I connect to music weirds some people out, but other people think it's cool. I have friends from a lot of places, but I don't belong anywhere. Sometimes, I eat Flaming Hot Cheetos for dinner. I might come from some darkness, but I choose to be a light. I try, anyway. Really hard. Honestly. Really hard.

This photo was taken by Brian Lee of Brian Lee Photography. What an amazing photo shoot! I feel beautiful.
https://www.facebook.com/brianleephotographybellevue/
Thanks, Brian!

www.ingramcontent.com/pod-product-compliance
Lightning Source LLC
Chambersburg PA
CBHW071406290426
44108CB00014B/1705